Tom Brady: MVP

Most Valuable Patriot

SPORTS PUBLISHING L.L.C

BOSTON HERALD

TOM BRADY: MVP

Most Valuable Patriot

SPORTS PUBLISHING L.L.C.

Publisher: Peter L. Bannon
Senior Managing Editors: Susan M. Moyer and Joseph J. Bannon Jr.
Art Director: K. Jeffrey Higgerson
Senior Graphic Designer: Kenneth J. O'Brien
Graphic Designers: Joseph Brumleve and Christine Mohrbacher
Imaging: Erin Linden-Levy
Developmental Editor: Stephanie Fuqua
Copy Editor: Cynthia L. McNew

BOSTON HERALD

President and Publisher: Patrick J. Purcell
Editor: Andrew F. Costello
Executive Sports Editor: Mark Torpey
Director of Photography: Garo Lachinian
Vice President/Promotion: Gwen Gage
Chief Librarian: John Cronin

All stories and photographs are from the files of the *Boston Herald*.
Front and back cover photos: Jim Mahoney

ISBN:1-58261-571-3

Printed in Mexico

Contents

Introduction

It was a story worthy of Hollywood's best sports scribes. Game two of the 2001 season. The veteran quarterback takes a hard hit late in the fourth quarter and leaves the stadium on a stretcher, bound for the hospital. Enter backup quarterback. Enter Tom Brady.

Some teams might have fallen apart without their veteran leader. Some backup quarterbacks might have found themselves not up to the task. But Brady was able to take this 0-2 team straight to a miraculous and unexpected Super Bowl victory.

Of course, there were a few bumps in the road. Brady's inexperience showed in game four against the Dolphins and again in game seven against the Broncos. Fans and media pundits endlessly argued the quarterback controversy of Bledsoe or Brady. But Brady was able to shake off those distractions and concentrate on the next game ahead of him. Again and again.

At the end of the journey, Brady found himself the Super Bowl MVP and a Pro Bowl pick, and a new voyage began. One of visits to Disney World and the White House, judging beauty contests and gracing the covers of magazines.

And once more, Brady mostly ignored the hype and focused his eye on next season and his next challenge: proving that he's no one-hit wonder.

Stephanie Fuqua
Developmental Editor

BRADY SHOWS BUNCH OF PROMISE

By Michael Felger

You may not see him for another year, may not even remember who he is by the time the Patriots' 2002 training camp rolls around. But Tom Brady will be here just the same, working on his game six days a week and wearing a headset and holding a clipboard on the seventh.

At some point down the line, Brady will get his chance. And when he does, he may surprise you.

Just like this summer.

The second-year quarterback was widely regarded as one of the Patriots' most improved players this preseason, so much so that the release of Michael Bishop two weeks ago barely created a ripple. The Pats signed Damon Huard in free agency this offseason to be Drew Bledsoe's primary backup, but when Bill Belichick was asked on Friday who his No. 2 guy was, the coach said that issue was still being evaluated.

Huard figures to be the choice in the short term, but Brady can't be far behind. Not after his play in the preseason, when he led all Patriots quarterbacks by completing 30 of 53 passes for 375 yards and two touchdowns with no interceptions.

Brady's play was an extension of the work he put in during the offseason, when he was a leader in the spring workout program. The 2000 sixth-round pick out of Michigan added 10-15 pounds of muscle to his 6-foot-4, 220-pound frame and immersed himself in Charlie Weis's offense. Brady came to camp ready to produce, and then he delivered.

Of all the Pats quarterbacks, Brady showed the most poise in the pocket and the most willingness to stand up against the rush and deliver the ball.

"I think it went pretty well, pretty much what I expected. I feel a lot more comfortable than I did last year," said Brady. "You get out there and you start to feel comfortable with everything, and when that happens your athletic ability takes over. You just start making better reads and better throws.

"I think the ball is just coming out faster. Quicker. I think I'm moving a little better, but I'm still working on that every day. There are so many things to improve on. I'm so far from where I want to be that I'm just trying to make that headway."

Brady's climb up the depth chart is nothing new. At Michigan, he was supposed to be the understudy to highly touted Drew Henson, but on Saturdays, Brady usually got the call. Brady bridged the gap in talent with smarts and leadership, just like he's doing now.

When Brady arrived in Foxboro last year, he was surprised to find out how many players didn't "get it." He was shocked by the lack of work ethic in some quarters and the poor attitudes in others. Guys just showing up. At Michigan, that wasn't tolerated.

Belichick was obviously on the same page, because he spent much of his offseason free agent spending spree on players who possess leadership, toughness and work ethic. Brady said the difference is already apparent.

"I think this is a different team from last year, just in terms of attitude," he said. "And that's all from the coaches. If we came back with the same attitude—first of all it's unprofessional—but second of all it doesn't get it done."

Brady's own attitude will remain strong even if he doesn't get one snap in the regular season. He knows his time will come.

"That's the role," he said. "You're a backup. In a way, you don't really want to have to go in because that means somebody got hurt. But I'm going to prepare every day like I am going to play—just like Damon will and just like Drew will. If that point comes, then I'm sure Damon and I will be able to step up to the challenge."

For now, Brady will earn even more experience by wearing a headset on game days and relaying the plays from coaching staff in to Bledsoe from the sidelines.

Wherever Brady ends up, Belichick is pleased with what he has at the position. Bledsoe is the marquee guy, Huard is a proven veteran who has won NFL games, and Brady is the up-and-comer.

Said Belichick, "I think that our quarterbacks through the course of training camp have shown to be one of the positions we have a little bit of depth at."

Backup Hears Call

By Mark Murphy

Tom Brady's alarm went off yesterday in fairly typical fashion for a backup quarterback.

With just over five minutes left in the Patriots' 10-3 loss to the New York Jets yesterday at Foxboro Stadium, Pats quarterback Drew Bledsoe was knocked out of bounds and short of a first down by Jets linebacker Mo Lewis while running for eight yards on third down. Lewis's hit made Brady wince.

"Like I told Damon [Huard] after that, if I got hit that hard, I would have been in the hospital for a month," Brady said.

Brady replaced Bledsoe two possessions after the hit, and while working the team's two-minute drill, he nearly drove the Pats into the end zone.

"Drew is such a fighter," Brady said. "He got hit as hard as anyone I've ever seen."

Patriots coach Bill Belichick also decided, based on Bledsoe's performance in a subsequent drive, that his starting quarterback was too dazed to continue. Though Brady played briefly in a game last season against the Detroit Lions, yesterday was his coming-out party.

And in the process of driving the Patriots 41 yards on a series of crisp medium passes, in addition to a nine-yard run to the sideline, Brady put the offense in a position to at least tie the game.

But his last two passes—the first a Hail Mary with eight seconds left that bounced off the hands of David Patten in the end zone, and the second an incompletion with two seconds left that bounced off a heavily covered Charles Johnson on the two-yard line—failed to convert.

"I just knew that we needed a touchdown," the second-year player said. "Those passes were close, a close call. But that's the sort of situation

you don't want to get into too often. I just aimed for the middle of the field, got four guys up there, and hoped that one of them could jump for it.

"Those aren't the situations you want, though. You're just trying to finish it off."

From Big Blue to Replacing Drew

By Mark Murphy

Lloyd Carr stumbled on the scene purely by accident.

The University of Michigan coach was walking down a hallway of the Wolverines' practice facility in Ann Arbor last Sunday, between meetings, when he noticed a group of assistants planted in front of a television watching the Patriots-Jets game.

Darned if that wasn't Tom Brady leading the Pats' offense downfield in a crisp, efficient and desperate two-minute drill. It came down to two passes—Brady's Hail Mary with eight seconds left that receiver David Patten couldn't quite grab, and another that bounced off the heavily covered Charles Johnson on the two-yard line with two seconds left.

Carr, as much as anyone in Foxboro Stadium in those last ten seconds, believed.

"Honest to goodness, I expected him to take them in," said Carr, the one man who perhaps more than anyone else had to be sold on the merits of Tom Brady.

Carr's evolution as a Brady fan took a long time. But it also culimated in Brady leading the Wolverines to one of the most stirring bowl performances in Michigan history—a 35-34 overtime win over Alabama in the 2000 Orange Bowl.

Beyond Brady's ability to cut Alabama apart with a 33 of 45 passing performance that included 344 yards and three touchdowns, it was the then-senior's response to a 14-0 deficit that Michigan quarterback coach Stan Parrish remembers most.

There were 58 seconds left in the first half when Michigan got the ball back, and Brady drove the team 44 yards. He completed all five passes, including a 27-yard strike that Parrish said turned the game around.

"We ran a deep option route with David Terrell," said Parrish.

"Now, Terrell broke it off, and Brady just stayed right there with him and got him the ball."

Carr said the Orange Bowl may have been the defining moment for Brady in a season in which the quarterback, despite the presence of Michigan's standard stock of NFL-bound talent, was named the team MVP.

"That was certainly an outstanding performance," Carr said of the Orange Bowl.

"But my favorite that season was the one at Penn State—down by ten points, with six minutes to go, Tom had thrown an interception that went back for a touchdown, and he takes us back on two incredible drives [for touchdown passes] where any mistake by a quarterback would have ended it."

Michigan won, 31-27. Ultimately, as every serious Brady fan at Michigan will point out, Brady won 20 games in his final two years as a starting quarterback.

But that success came only after Brady, in a moment of doubt, nearly transferred. And only after he made the difficult choice to remain, despite the fact that the more celebrated Brian Griese had risen ahead of him early on.

Though Brady is now in the midst of his second pro year, enjoyed a strong 2001 preseason, and efficiently stepped in for Drew Bledsoe and ran the two-minute drill last Sunday, Pats fans probably won't know what to expect when the 24-year-old Bay Area native makes his first NFL start against the Colts today.

But for those familiar with his decisions—in every part of life—nothing should be surprising.

Choosing the Tough Route

From Brian Griese to Tom Brady to Yankees phenom Drew Henson, the Carr/

Parrish axis has turned out a remarkable succession of NFL-ready quarterback talent in Ann Arbor. Beneath this success story, however, lies a faceless cast of second-, third- and even fourth—string quarterbacks who spent their time straining for a glimpse of light at the top of the depth chart.

For Brady, that initially meant competing not only with Griese, but also with Scott Driesenbach, a talented quarterback who, like Griese, arrived in Ann Arbor a

year ahead of Brady in 1995. Initially, Brady saw himself struggling to reach the surface. A year after his own arrival, the much-touted Henson checked in.

"You DO have to compete here," said Carr.

Indeed, Tom Brady Sr. remembers when his son, who was recruited out of Serra High School in San Mateo by nearby University of Califonia with the offer of playing almost immediately, chose a tough, uphill road over the easy one.

For a family that did everything together—from their season tickets at 49ers games to watching the progress of three older daughters who excelled in varsity sports at local state universities—the younger Tom's college choice was a daunting shot of the unknown.

"Cal told him that he could start as a sophomore, junior and senior, and Michigan said, 'We already have six quarterbacks,'' said the elder Brady, a 57-year-old employee benefits manager. "My choice for him would have been Cal. It was right down the street, and one of his older sisters had gone there. But it would have been handed to him. He just felt that this is what he wanted."

Determined to Succeed

Brady, after getting into two games in his first year at Michigan, redshirted the rest of his freshman season. Then he started to do the math, weigh what seemed to be a cool reception by Carr, and worry.

"What happened was that Brian Griese and Tom were competing for the same job," said Carr. "At the time, [Driesenbach] was the starter, Griese was the backup, and Tom was third string. He

started to think about transferring, because Griese had two years of eligibility left and the other guy had three. I told him that he was probably being premature about it, but that he should talk to his dad and then come back to me.

"He came back the next morning and said, 'Coach, I'm going to prove to you that I'm the best quarterback you have, and I'm going to stay here.'"

The first, and most important, response from Tom and Galynn Brady was to simply offer unconditional support.

"He felt it to the depths of his heart," said the elder Brady. "He came to the point where he said, 'I hate what's going on, but I won't let this beat me.' The decision to stay there and succeed was the biggest one that he could have made. We were behind 100 percent of whatever he was going to want, but he was 20, and it was going to be his decision if he left Michigan."

That fiery spirit would seem to belie one of Brady's most noticeable traits: his calmness. It marked his performance after stepping in for Bledsoe last Sunday, just as it colored his postgame demeanor.

Thinking back last week to that freshman dilemma, Brady's voice remained quiet, albeit with a trace of what Carr calls Brady's "inner fire" flashing out.

"I just made the decision not to let that bother me," Brady said. "I think I'm just comfortable with what I can do. Coming from Michigan, I've already played in front of 112,000 people. That helps you to deal with a lot of pressure."

And then there was Carr's own unique lesson in pressure.

"Lloyd Carr has a goal of perfection," said the elder Brady. "Anything less is unacceptable. And Lloyd became one of his biggest fans, because Tom doesn't make many mistakes. It was pretty satisfying to be elected first-team captain, and then team MVP, when you have so many MVPs on your team."

A Diamond in the Rough?

And Brady was taken by the Pats in the sixth round of the 2000 draft. Consider the following predraft report on Brady by

Pro Football Weekly:

Negatives: Poor build. Very skinny and narrow. Ended the '99 season weighing 195 pounds and still looks like a rail at 211. Looks a little frail and lacks great physical stature and strength. Can get pushed down more easily than you'd like.

This theme continued for several more lines. Brady's positives were listed in terms of intangibles and decision-making.

And to those who watched Brady develop from a kid who even had to fight for the starting quarterback job at Serra High, this apparent case of underestimation is merely history repeating itself.

And, oh, yes. The 6-foot-4 Brady has since "bulked" up to 220 pounds, which is hardly the point.

"He's one of my all-time favorites here, because he's even a better person than he is a player, but Tom is a tough guy," said Parrish. "I don't like seeing anyone get hurt, but I know Tom is going to do exactly what he has to [in taking over for Bledsoe]. He wasn't drafted particularly high, but neither was Griese."

Carr, however, admits that he was left at a loss on draft day 2000.

"Yeah, I was surprised, especially when you look at what he did when he was here," Carr said of Brady. "Henson, if he had come out to play football, would have been taken in the top two or three picks. But Tom fought him off while he was here. Brady is the ultimate competitor.

"Personally, I think it was a great selection by the Patriots, and I think he'll prove that. He's a really bright kid. He and Brian Griese are as bright as they come. He's not just a guy who wants to throw passes. He takes the intelligence part of the game very seriously. He's not a loud guy, but he has a tremendous intensity.

"When you're the quarterback at Michigan, there are always going to be people who question something. But he moved through it very well."

As he always does. Brady's father admits that he's biased, but then again, he's proud of that bias. It has a way of spreading to anyone who spends more than a season with his son.

"He's never been revered," said the elder Brady. "His attitude, after he was drafted, was that the Patriots were lucky to get him at that point in the draft. His method is that he may not be the best, but he'll outwork everyone else.

"When I talked to him about [today's] game, his attitude was, 'This is all right. I've been through this before. I'm not at all nervous.'"

Understudy Acts Like Leading Man

By Mark Murphy

Tom Brady looked up, saw the Michigan football jersey, and knew where to turn for reassurance while making his first NFL start. Brady's two older sisters, Maureen and Julie, were sitting in the Foxboro Stadium stands yesterday, with one wearing the former Wolverine's college colors.

Before long, though, Drew Bledsoe's replacement as the Patriots' starting quarterback didn't need much reassurance. Things went that well for the second-year QB during a 44-13 win over the Indianapolis Colts.

Brady finished 13 of 23 passing for 168 yards, was sacked only once for an 11-yard loss, and lived up to a trait that he established during his last two years at Michigan: he took care of the ball and didn't make mistakes.

He may have been making his NFL starting debut, but Brady obviously wasn't whistling past an early grave last week when he told his father that he wasn't nervous.

"I've always had high expectations for myself," Brady said. "I set my goals high. I've been prepared for this. It's not as if they pulled me off the street and said, 'You're starting.'"

Instead, Brady got word that he would be the Pats' starter while Drew Bledsoe was being driven to the hospital last Sunday for what turned out to be a four-night stay with internal injuries. Bledsoe's mere presence along the Patriots' sideline yesterday, albeit in street clothes, could not have been more important to his understudy.

"Drew said the most important thing was to go out there and have fun, because you're as prepared as you're going to be at that point," Brady said. "I talked to Drew [Saturday] night, and asked him how he thought [the Colts' defense] would play. He said they would probably be conservative, play the run and blitz, and that's pretty much what they did.

"This was just a good start [yesterday]."

And save for sailing his second pass over the head of his intended receiver, Brady settled in and led the Patriots to their first win of 2001.

"The ball just jumped," he said. "He was wide open. You have to make those throws. But everyone just told me to get the next one, and that's the approach you have to take out there."

Judging by the 44-13 win, Brady took the right approach.

Welcoming Added Pressure

By Michael Felger

Tom Brady knows that life as a New England Patriot will probably never be the same.

And he's more than ready for it.

From his days at Michigan, Brady knows what it's like to be in the spotlight. Having played behind Brian Griese and ahead of Drew Henson, he's more than familiar with quarterback controversies. He's uniquely qualified to handle the off-field distractions.

Brady is facing all of that right now, as the second-year pro takes the reins from Drew Bledsoe while Bledsoe recovers from internal injuries. Last Sunday, Brady responded by leading the Pats to a blowout victory over Indianapolis. This week, it gets much tougher with a date in Miami.

Yesterday, standing at the podium that has been occupied by Bledsoe for most of the past nine years, Brady was asked how he's adjusting to going from the shadows to center stage.

"The biggest thing is that I don't have as much free time," said Brady. "Things like this. Usually I'd be eating lunch right now. [There's] also the phone calls and that type of stuff. The preparation is the same. It's more the off-field stuff, just a little less free time. Which is fine, because I like being busy."

One distraction Brady won't allow is the talk among fans and the media over whether he or Bledsoe should be the starting quarterback. Brady learned that lesson with the Wolverines, when he and highly touted local prospect Henson battled for playing time.

Brady's approach earned him most of the snaps in his final two seasons and a 20-5 record as a starter for Michigan—including a 2-0 record at the site of this Sunday's game, Miami's Pro Player Stadium.

"That goes on at every level, and it's something that I've been a part of," said Brady, the Pats' sixth-round pick in the 2000 draft. "And the one approach that works for me is, I just control my performance. And if that's good enough, then that's good enough. And if they say play, I play. And if they say don't play, I don't play.

"That's just comforting to me, and I sleep better at night knowing that I've done what I can do. And the rest is left up to other people who are making the decisions."

As was apparent last week against the Colts, Brady is a different quarterback than Bledsoe. While both are drop-back pocket passers, Brady appears to have a greater comfort level with the short and intermediate throws. For a player of his limited experience, Brady also has impressive poise in the pocket and against the rush. He may not be able to hit the big plays that Bledsoe can, but he'll still move the chains.

"My style is my style," said Brady. "If I see a chance to take a shot, I'll take the shot. If you don't see it, you dump it."

Coach Bill Belichick has said that the game plan hasn't changed significantly since Brady took over. What may be different, however, is the size of the game plan. According to several players, the playbook for the Colts game was far smaller than the

one used the previous week against the Jets.

It appears the Pats will be able to keep it simple against Miami as well, as the Dolphins, according to Belichick, "are not big into [defensive] disguise and deception. They line up and say, here we are, come get us."

Brady is hoping to do just that.

Following Milloy's Lead

By Kevin Mannix

When the Patriots locker room opened about ten minutes after their 30-10 pounding by the Dolphins yesterday, most of the players were either entering or exiting the shower area. Most of them, anyway.

Quarterback Tom Brady was still sitting in front of his locker in full uniform. Sitting beside him was Lawyer Milloy, who had made a quick detour to talk with the youngster. When their conversation ended, Milloy stood and gave Brady an encouraging tap on the head.

Feel the kid needed some encouragement, Lawyer?

"Not at all," Milloy said. "In fact, he pulled me aside. Tom's a leader. He was already thinking about what we need to do. Tom's a leader. He's not a captain but he is a leader because of the position he plays. As a quarterback, he's an honorary captain. We'll rally around him because he's a leader in my eyes."

Milloy said Brady's message involved the team's preparation.

"He told me [yesterday's loss] started on Wednesday, when we began practicing," said Milloy, a defensive co-captain. "I know the point he was making. I told him that if he sees guys are messing up on offense to feel free to come to me. I'll stop the drill, bring the team up and start over.

"He needs to realize that we'll rally around him."

Brady insists there was no big deal to his discussion.

"Just two teammates talking," he said. "I just said that I thought we need to take a different approach every day, not just on Sunday. I hate to lose and the fact is, you can't practice average on Wednesday and Thursday and okay on Friday and expect to play well on Sunday.

"But if you practice great on Wednesday and Thursday, there's no reason not to play great on Sunday," Brady added. "That's the only approach I know how to take. We need to start getting things done [during practice] every day so there's no reason to come out and play like we did today."

If the quarterback was disappointed in the way the team prepared, why not say something during the week? Why wait until after the game?

"It wasn't like I walked off the field on Wednesday and Thursday thinking, 'God, we practiced bad.' It's an overall feeling. If we miss a play on Wednesday, it's like, 'Okay, we'll get it corrected by Thursday.'

"Then we never get back to it. You never think that because you don't practice well on Wednesday, you're not going to play well. But that's the approach we have to take. We've got to shoot for practicing great. We need to be better all around, and that starts with practice.

"It's a matter of execution and focus. You shouldn't have the approach of getting through practice on Wednesday or Thursday to get to the game. You have to execute in practice to prove to yourself and the coaches that when those situations come up in the game, you'll be able to execute."

Brady pointed to his own performance during the week as a prime example.

"Sometimes in practice, I'll miss a guy who's open and I'll just say, 'How did I miss him?' That's the kind of thing I have to change. I've got to concentrate more on making the right passes in practice. I have to sharpen that up. If you're not making completions in practice, why should you wonder why you miss guys on Sunday?"

Having that approach is fine, but why the need to talk with Milloy about it?

"Because I look on him as a team leader," Brady explained. "Watching him play, I can see that the game means a lot to him. He puts it all out there and performs great. I've looked up to him since I came here, and I know he's one of several guys the team listens to.

"Lawyer knows my attitude," Brady added.

"I think we have a connection, and I feel very comfortable with him. He's a friend, and he wanted to hear what I had to say."

Brady in Control

By Michael Felger

Tom Brady performed so well in Sunday's 29-26 overtime win over San Diego that it's hard to know where to start. Perhaps a career statistic will serve as a good jumping-off point:

Brady has yet to throw an NFL interception. Even in preseason.

Given the state of the Patriots' offensive line, the team's suspect receiving corps and the amount of mistakes being made around him, it's mind-boggling that Brady has thrown the ball 114 times in the regular season and hasn't had one picked off. The fact only underscores Brady's greatest strength: He doesn't make many mistakes.

That was certainly the case Sunday. Brady put the ball in the air 54 times and never came close to an interception, despite constant outside pressure from Chargers defensive ends Raylee Johnson and Marcellus Wiley and inside heat from linebacker Junior Seau.

"The things I liked the best about his performance were his decisions with the ball—I thought he was going to the right place most of the time," coach Bill Belichick said. "I thought he showed a lot of poise under pressure, stepping up into the pocket."

Meanwhile, Brady did most of the little things well. Start with his cadence at the line of scrimmage. The Pats coaches knew Seau and the Chargers would try to rattle Brady by jumping up on top of the ball during the snap count. Brady countered that with a few hard counts, and the result was three encroachment penalties on the Chargers, two of which gave the Pats a first down.

Given the fact that the 24-year-old Brady has played only four NFL games, his command at the line and in the huddle was amazing. Nowhere was it more evident than during the Pats' first offensive play of overtime, when Brady picked up an interior blitz, checked to a play with maximum protection and then lofted a bomb to receiver David Patten. The play drew a pass interference call to set up Adam Vinatieri's game-winning field goal.

"They were bringing the house," center Damien Woody said. "He checked to max-protect and got it done. I've been saying all along, he doesn't play like an inexperienced quarterback. He saw there was a situation and he put us in position to take advantage of it."

As has been the case over and over with Brady, preparation was the key. The Pats, knowing the Chargers preferred that blitz, worked on that pickup all week at practice. Then, at the most crucial moment, Brady went to it.

"It shows the type of character the guy has," Patten said. "With the game on the line like that, it just shows he's out there to make it happen."

Airing Out Patriots Offense

By Rich Thompson

The Patriots' 38-17 victory Sunday over the Indianapolis Colts convinced coach Bill Belichick that his team is a bona fide air power in the NFL.

Quarterback Tom Brady enjoyed his second straight mistake-free effort, and the Patriots are 3-1 since he replaced incumbent Drew Bledsoe. Brady was named NFL Player of the Week last week for completing 33 of 54 passes for 364 yards and two touchdowns in the Patriots' 29-26 overtime victory over the San Diego Chargers on Oct. 14 at Foxboro Stadium.

Brady didn't duplicate those numbers against the Colts, but he orchestrated quick-strike drives that kept the pressure on Peyton Manning and the Colts' powerful offense. Brady completed 16 of 20 passes to five different receivers for 202 yards and two touchdowns. Brady set a Patriots record with a 91-yard touchdown pass to David Patten.

"I think offensively, the passing game is starting to look like an NFL passing game," Belichick said. "The receivers are getting open, the quarterback is getting the ball to the receivers when they are open and they are getting it.

"The distribution has been better on the routes so that their openings are created. I think overall, our pass protection has improved in the last month."

Patriots tight end Jermaine Wiggins has been on the business end of Brady touchdown passes against the Chargers and the Colts. Brady has found Wiggins to be a reliable receiver in short yardage near the goal line. Wiggins's 3-yard catch against San Diego with 36 seconds on the clock forced overtime. He recorded his second TD against the Colts with 1:17 to play in the half that gave the Patriots a 28-3 lead.

Wiggins approves of Brady's share-the-wealth philosophy and said it has facilitated the Patriots' upsurge in the NFL's air wars.

"We are trying to spread it out, and every week somebody makes big plays; that's what we are going for," Wiggins said. "David Patten had a big game, Terry Glenn had a big game last week and Troy Brown was big in both. What it comes down to is having different guys have big games. When everybody is being utilized, it creates a better offense in general because nobody can key on just one guy."

Patten has been a direct beneficiary of Brady's largesse with the football. Patten caught seven passes for 73 yards against the Chargers and added four catches for 117 yards and two TDs against the Colts.

Despite his individual success against the Colts, Patten credited the club's recent success to Brady's command of Charlie Weis's playbook.

"Brady is getting the opportunity to do what we knew he could do all along, and he's been doing it since training camp," Patten said. "You

can't say enough about the kid. We're up 21-3 and he comes in the huddle and says, 'Let's keep going.' He's a true leader."

Brown has faced double coverage since being elevated to the top of the depth chart. But with the return of Glenn against the Chargers and Patten's effort against the Colts, defenses can no longer focus on taking Brown out of the game.

"The best way to be successful is to have a bunch of guys on the field that can make plays," Brown said.

Facing a Crucial Test

By Kevin Mannix

Now we'll find out about Tom Brady. It was too early to make a judgment when he took the NFL by storm during the Patriots' recent 3-1 run. It's also too early to call him a one-month wonder after his disastrous fourth-quarter performance in yesterday's 31-20 loss to the Broncos at Invesco Field.

It's not too early, however, to realize that the heat is on. He insists he's still confident in his ability. His coach said that. But there may be some doubting Patriots in the locker room, and they'll be looking to see how he rebounds next week in Atlanta.

Former coach Bill Parcells always used to say that you can't tell how good a player is until he's been hit in the mouth a couple of times. How he responds to that adversity would tell a coach plenty about any player. After the game, Drew Bledsoe basically said the same thing, telling the second-year quarterback, "This is where you show what you're made of."

After a relatively seamless transition into the NFL in his first four starts, Brady got smacked around pretty good in the fourth. He didn't throw an interception in his first 162 passes as a Patriot, only to throw four interceptions in 14 pass attempts in the final quarter. One came in the Broncos' end zone, ending the Pats' final chance to take the lead. Another was returned 39 yards for a touchdown for the final score of the game.

The bottom line: Brady completed 100 passes in 155 attempts for 1,029 yards and seven touchdowns with no interceptions going into yesterday's final quarter. In that one quarter, he completed as many passes to the Broncos as he did to his teammates. His fourth-quarter numbers were absolutely abysmal, finishing 4 of 14 for 40 yards with four interceptions and a sack.

Toughness and resilience are allegedly two of Brady's primary attributes. Now is his chance to prove it to Patriots players and fans, because he's got a lot of rebounding to do after struggling through what was arguably the worst quarter of football ever played by a Patriots quarterback.

"You can't miss throws like I did out there," he said. "I'd been making those throws before. I've got to do a better job of communicating with the receivers. I'm the checks and balances guy out there, so when there is a mix-up it's my fault. Every week I learn something new, and this is just another step in the process. I've never thrown four interceptions in a game before, so coming back from this will be really tough. We just need to be more precise in the passing game."

The only encouraging word came from head coach Bill Belichick.

"I thought Tom played pretty well," Belichick said. "He was trying to get the ball into the end zone, but it didn't work out."

Brady wasn't about to let himself off the hook.

"I've got to do a lot better job knowing where the receivers are going to be," he said.

That's probably a universal lament among young quarterbacks, but few of them had the kind of start that Brady enjoyed in his first four games as a starter. Over that time, you could count the bad throws he made on one hand and still have a couple free. In the fourth quarter yesterday, everything unraveled. He and his receivers had the dreaded "failure to communicate" more in that 15 minutes than in the previous games combined.

On his first pick at the end of the Pats' first series in the fourth quarter, he was rolling to his right and committed the sin of throwing back to the middle of the field. Denard Walker was step for step with David Patten as he crossed under the goal post coming in Brady's direction and stepped right in front of Patten for the interception.

"That's a throw I've got to put in a place where, if David doesn't catch it, nobody else will," he said.

Realizing your mistake is a good first step. The tough part will be correcting it. In the meantime, however, it's probably time to stop wondering what the Pats can get in a trade for Bledsoe.

Rebounding from Denver

By Karen Guregian

The postscript from last week's loss in Denver read like a soap opera cliffhanger regarding Patriots quarterback Tom Brady. After throwing four interceptions in the fourth quarter of the Broncos loss, the fate of our fair Brady was left dangling until this week.

Would he buckle or wouldn't he? Would he respond favorably against the Falcons or would we get more of the same? Would the quarterback controversy pick up steam or fizzle out for good?

From fans, to teammates, to coaches, to the Patriots Faithful—many of whom made the trip south to the Georgia Dome and were a vocal presence at the game— they were all eager to find out how he would respond to his first real dose of adversity since taking over for the injured Drew Bledsoe.

Let's just say Brady proved one tough customer. He passed his first true test in the big leagues.

He just played like the Brady we've come to know during the past month and change—save for two hellacious quarters in Denver. He was calm and cool and stepped up in the pocket when needed to connect on 21 of 31 passes for 250 yards. He threw for three touchdowns and didn't hit a Falcons defender in the bunch. He wasn't picked off at all in yesterday's impressive 24-10 victory.

He also had a hand in the Patriots' version of the Immaculate Reception, as one of his third-quarter throws caromed off Atlanta cornerback Ashley Ambrose and flew back about 10 yards into the hands of Troy Brown, who ran 22 yards into the end zone.

So yes, Brady got lucky on one throw, but for the most part, he did his job and did it well. There was one stretch from late in the first quarter through the second where he hit 11 straight passes. You also won't find a better drive than the one Brady engineered with 2:56 left before the half, moving the team 89 yards on 10 plays, culminating with a TD toss to Marc Edwards.

"It was hugely important [to see how he'd respond]," Brown said. "Like I said last week, it was going to be a big test for him. It was the first time he faced adversity like that after having a bad game . . . and he bounced back like the Tom Brady we know."

Brady certainly erased a lot of the doubt that crept in during the past week. Some people might have thought he was headed deeper into the has-been pile when his first throw of the game sailed high and wide of David Patten and his second throw missed Patrick Pass over the middle.

Once he got into a rhythm, once he got his technique down, he was lights out, particularly in the second quarter when he completed 15 of 17 passes for 150 yards and two touchdowns. He couldn't have delivered a better lob fade over the head of Falcons linebacker Keith Brooking to hit Kevin Faulk with his first TD throw.

Typically, the dimple-chinned quarterback downplayed the significance of yesterday's outing in terms of his personal growth. He did his best not to personalize the matter at all, speaking mostly in terms of the team as opposed to his own trials and tribulations.

He claimed he didn't feel any added pressure to prove himself. He maintained the four interceptions didn't rattle him. In fact, he couldn't get back on the field soon enough for his taste.

"There's been hard times before that I've had," Brady said. "You learn how to deal with them and just move forward. Sometimes you come out in a game like this and you just got to put everything behind you and move forward. 'Cuz you can't get last week back."

Well, then he moved forward in a big way. The two wins he quarterbacked over Indianpolis as well as the come-from-behind victory over San Diego were impressive. Nothing was more important than what he showed yesterday. He wasn't over-eager, trying to right the wrongs of Denver, or timid, afraid to make throws for fear of making a gaffe. He was just Tom Brady, the godsend of an understudy who has the Patriots back in business.

Taking His Medicine

By Ed Gray

When Tom Brady stepped to the podium at yesterday's postgame press conference, the second-year Patriots quarterback couldn't believe his eyes.

"Where is everyone?" asked Brady, giving way to a sheepish smirk that made clear he knew why the interview room was scattered with reporters and cameramen after the Pats' sloppy 21-11 win over the Buffalo Bills.

Brady had grown accustomed to the media circus surrounding his first six games as the starter, but his rough day yesterday hardly warranted a standing-room-only crowd.

"It's always good getting a 'W.' That's what I'm always concerned about," said the 23-year-old Michigan product, whose father, Tom Sr., was in attendance yesterday. "You obviously like to go out and play good every week, but that's not always the case in this league, as I'm finding out."

For those interested in how the upstart quarterback came back to earth after impressively leading the Pats to a 4-2 record in relief of the injured Drew Bledsoe, Brady did not make excuses for a performance during which he was sacked seven times and fumbled twice.

"With the sacks I've had, I'm really going to focus on where I'm looking [to avoid them]. Sometimes you're looking in the wrong place, and that's what gets sacks. Sometimes you're looking in the right place, and they're just doing a good job of covering," said Brady.

Brady was most upset with fumbling while being sacked by defensive end Kendrick Office with 3:04 left in the game. Linebacker Jay Foreman recovered the ball on the Pats' 17-yard line and the Bills then pulled within three points two plays later when Alex Van Pelt, subbing for the injured Rob Johnson, connected with Peerless Price for a 17-yard touchdown and Eric Moulds for a subsequent two-point conversion.

"I was looking inside to David [Patten] and I just saw a whole lot of bodies in there," Brady said of the fumble play. "The last second, I saw a guy flash and he just got his hand on the ball. That's careless. When somebody

swipes at the ball, it's going to come out if it's not secure. That's the most frustrating play of the day for me. I just have to improve on that, man."

Though Brady had an off day, completing just 15 of 21 passes with one touchdown and one interception, he still had to field a question about the quarterback controversy that his sharp play has created.

"I'm just concerned with how I'm playing. I'll let Drew be concerned about how he feels and when he's ready to go," he said. "I don't know when he's coming back, and all I know is I'm going to keep playing as hard as I can."

Same Name, Different Game

By Steve Buckley

Ever since that painful Sunday afternoon when a ruthless hit from Jets linebacker Mo Lewis landed Drew Bledsoe in a hospital bed at Massachusetts General Hospital, Tom Brady has been at the center of a real live quarterback controversy.

In one corner, we have the Bledsoe supporters, who believe the veteran quarterback—deemed healthy again by the medical professionals—should get his old job back. In the other corner, we have a new frontier of Brady supporters who simply point to the numbers: The Pats are 5-2 since The Kid took over at quarterback.

However the controversy turns out, Brady, for now, is an instant celebrity. We've dissected and analyzed every pass he's thrown - every completion ("He's a real find!"), every touchdown ("He's a future Hall of Famer!"), every interception ("Bring back Bledsoe!"). We've looked back to his college days at Michigan. We're on a first-name basis with the fetching Brady sisters. And, thanks to a hilarious piece produced by ESPN, we've even given you a very Brady fantasy: Young Tom as the outcast fourth son in "The Brady Bunch."

But now, in the interest of keeping the home fires burning and giving you yet more information on the Patriots' 24-year-old quarterback, we present "Tom Brady: Baseball Player."

"Everyone loves tall, left-handed hitting catchers, and that's what I was," Brady said. "I'm happy with the way things are turning out in football, but sometimes I do wonder what might have happened if I chose to play baseball."

Most Patriots fans are aware that Brady played hardball during his days at Serra High School in San Mateo, Calif., and that in 1995, near the end of his senior year, he was selected by the Montreal Expos in the 18th round of the June amateur draft. What most Patriots fans do not know is that Brady was so highly regarded a high school catcher that he probably would have been taken considerably earlier in the draft were it not for the fact that he had stated his intentions to play football at Michigan.

"A lot of teams backed off from him for that reason," said Pete Jensen, Brady's baseball coach at Serra High. "The Expos took a flier on him, hoping they could convince him to sign, I guess. He was solid—the best catch-and-throw guy I've ever had. Good defensive catcher, good hitter, good attitude. I'll tell you this: I'm one of the few high school coaches who lets the catcher call his own game, and Tom was better than all of them at that. He ran the game."

In Barry's Footsteps

The baseball program at Serra is a well-oiled machine and an annual contender in the acclaimed Western Catholic Athletic League. The Padres have prepared many players for professional baseball careers, including Gregg Jeffries, longtime big-league manager Jim Fregosi, and Serra's greatest baseball player ever, Barry Bonds. Long before he set a single-season home run record with the San Francisco Giants, Bonds, Class of '82, was a baseball, basketball and football star at Serra.

But Bonds chose baseball, accepting a scholarship to play for the legendary Jim Brock at Arizona State. Brady, despite all the attention he received as a baseball player ("Sometimes there'd be 15 scouts watching him," said Jensen), chose football—and a scholarship at Michigan.

Why? To hear Brady tell it, it was because baseball is too ... rough.

"My elbow was always hurting me, my knees were always hurting me," he said. "It just seemed that after every game I'd have all the ice packs on my elbow and knees ..."

Informed of the lunacy of that statement—THE KID CHOSE COLLEGE FOOTBALL BECAUSE BASEBALL IS TOO ROUGH—Brady just laughed.

"Well, I *was* a catcher," he said. "And I think to be a good baseball player, I would have had to play in all the summer leagues, like the other guys were doing. There were guys who'd be playing 60 games in a summer in these different leagues, and I was always away at football camps. I didn't see any way I could do both."

But Brady understood the tug of baseball. As he put it, "Football is big in California, but baseball is bigger. If you were any good in sports, you played base-ball."

During Brady's two years on the Serra varsity, he appeared in 61 games, hitting .311 with eight home runs, 11 doubles and 44 RBIs. He was all-league catcher his senior year, and even though he had made it clear he was going to Michigan to play football, a trail of big-league scouts showed up at his games.

The one game that stands out—and Brady still talks about it to this day—was the showdown against Bellarmine Prep of San Jose. The Bells have always been Serra's archrivals in baseball, so it must have been that much sweeter for Brady to hit two home runs, throw out a runner trying to steal second and slam down the tag on a runner trying to score—all of it adding up to a 3-1 victory for the Padres.

"In between the home runs, they intentionally walked me," Brady said, the tone of his voice suggesting he's still a little miffed about the free pass. "I think the first home run tied the game, and the second home run put us ahead."

It was that game, according to Jensen, that transformed the Michigan-bound football player into a possible minor-league baseball player. More and more scouts began attending Serra baseball games, and now they were asking questions. Is he tough? Is he smart? Is he a problem kid?

"The only problem I ever had with Tom," said Jensen, "is that once in a while I just had to grab him and calm him down. He was so competitive, so intense, that he was always hard on himself. He expected to get a hit every time he was up, and if he didn't, or if he went 0 for 4, he wouldn't take it well.

"We had to reinforce to him that it was what he was doing in addition to the bat that helped us win games," Jensen said. "He was a field leader. He'd have been a big-league catcher for 15 years."

The Sticking Point

In the days leading up to the 1995 June amateur draft, it's reasonable to assume that many big-league teams crossed Brady off their shopping list. He was going to play football. He had the full boat waiting for him at Michigan. Why waste a draft pick on a college football player?

But in the 18th round, the Expos made their selection: Tom Brady, catcher, Serra High School.

The selection of Brady came three picks after the Dodgers picked Northeast-ern University pitcher Jay O'Shaughnessy. In that same round, the Red Sox selected a first baseman/outfielder from Puerto Rico named Felipe Roman.

Brady hesitated—just for a bit. Maybe it was a chance to take batting practice at Candlestick Park that temporarily put things on hold.

"The Expos were in San Francisco to play the Giants, and they invited Tom to work out with the team," recalled Brady's mother, Galynn. "We were all very excited. It was fun watching him take practice with the big-league players."

Did the Expos think they had a chance to land Brady?

"The makeup to this kid was just off the chart," said Dave Littlefield, now general manager of the Pittsburgh Pirates, who at the time served as a national cross-checker for the Expos. "He had the physical talent, but he was [also] smart, he hustled, came from a good family; we were impressed with everything we had heard about him."

But Littlefield also understood the lure of football. During his own schoolboy days, Littlefield was a football/baseball star at Portland (Maine) High School. A catcher, he chose to play minor-league ball with the Phillies. When his baseball career fizzled, he took advantage of a newly passed NCAA rule that allowed athletes to play professionally in one sport, and at the collegiate level in another sport. He played football at the University of Massachusetts and then embarked on a career in baseball administration.

"The talent levels were obviously different," Littlefield said, "but I know what it's like to have to make that decision. With Brady, we did get to investigate how much it would take to sign him, and we did talk about a significant amount of money. ... But the family just felt so inclined for the kid to go to school that we never got down to the hard-core negotiating."

Looking back over his old scouting reports, Littlefield remembers two things about Brady's visit to Candlestick Park. One, he hit a couple of home runs during batting practice. And two, "He came into the clubhouse after BP, and we were impressed with how he interacted with the big-league players, which is saying a lot for a high school player."

Still Taking His Cuts

Brady never played baseball again. Asked about the possibility of playing baseball during his collegiate days at Michigan, he said, "You really don't do that there."

But Brady retains an interest in baseball. He watched this year's gripping World Series between the Yankees and Arizona Diamondbacks. And it's not uncommon for Brady to wear a San Francisco Giants cap during his postgame press conferences, because "I'm a huge Giants fan."

And while he no longer plays competitive baseball, he's still taking his hacks.

"The batting cages up by the Funway Cafe, near the stadium—I've stopped in there a few times," Brady said. "I still like to swing the bat."

And though Brady turned away from baseball because he was tired of all those ice packs on his elbow and knees, at least one person—his mother—sometimes wonders if he made the right choice.

"As long as he's happy, that's all that matters," said Galynn Brady. But then, in a page right out of Mom 101, she added, "It's just that football is rough. I always worry about him getting hurt."

Finally Playing Like a Rookie

By Kevin Mannix

Is the wunderkind developing warts? That was the question for much of the Patriots game last night. For three quarters, Tom Brady looked like a rookie again, making mental and physical mistakes and failing to make plays when they were needed.

Even worse, he made mistakes at the worst times. While Antowain Smith's fumble inside the Rams' 5-yard line was unquestionably the turning point in the game, Brady's second interception resulted in significant damage to the Pats' chances as well.

That came in the middle of the third quarter, with the Pats trailing only 14-10. They got the ball and momentum after Kurt Warner bobbled a snap that was recovered by Pats linebacker Larry Izzo at the Rams' 45.

Time to make a couple of plays. Time to show a national TV audience what Bradymania is all about. Time to put the Pats in the upper echelon of NFL teams.

It didn't work out quite that way. On the first play after Izzo's recovery, Brady made two of the mistakes he's generally avoided this season: He threw the ball off-balance and into traffic.

With pressure coming at him up the middle, he didn't have a chance to step into the throw but made the pass anyway. Not a good thing. The ball was intended for Troy Brown but fell short and was picked off by Rams linebacker London Fletcher at the Rams' 40. He returned it 18 yards to the Pats' 42. Six plays later, Jeff Wilkins knocked through a 35-yard field goal to push the Rams' lead to 17-10.

At halftime Brady was 10 of 12 but for only 82 yards with one interception, a good pass that bounced off Kevin Faulk's hands right to Dexter McCleon at the Pats' 18. After three quarters, Brady had completed 14 of 22 for 120 yards with two interceptions.

Brady's night wasn't totally filled with short passes, however. After the Rams extended their lead to 24-10 following a 75-yard drive at the start of the fourth quarter, Brady took advantage of some passive Rams defense to get the Pats back in the game.

With St. Louis back in coverage, Brady completed five straight passes for 65 yards and a touchdown. There was a 15-yarder to Troy Brown, a 27-yarder to David Patten, a 2-yard dump to Charles Johnson, an 11-yard completion to Faulk, and, finally, a 10-yard pass to Patten in the back of the end zone, making it 24-17.

That was it, however. He and the offense never got the ball again as the Rams killed off the final seven minutes and 46 seconds of the game.

Thanks to the last drive, Brady's numbers weren't bad: 19 completions in 27 attempts for 185 yards with one touchdown and those two interceptions. Decent enough on paper. Better than last week when the Bills sacked him seven times and held him to an obscene 2.5 yards per pass attempt.

But not nearly enough to win a game against a good team like the Rams, the elite of the NFL. Particularly when the running game gained only 51 yards on 20 carries

and the offense was totally dependent on Brady and the receivers.

"They're a good team, and it's hard to beat a good team when you make mistakes like we did," Brady said after the game. "I thought we moved the ball OK. It wasn't like they stopped us. We were stopping ourselves with mistakes and didn't convert on third down like we need to."

Despite the loss and the problems the offense encountered, Brady insisted that this wasn't the end of the Patriots for the season.

"We played against a real good team and were right there with them," he said. "They were 7-1 and we had a chance to tie the game at the end. People can say what they want about the New England Patriots, but this defense is good enough to keep us in every game. Now the offense has to take advantage of what the defense gives us."

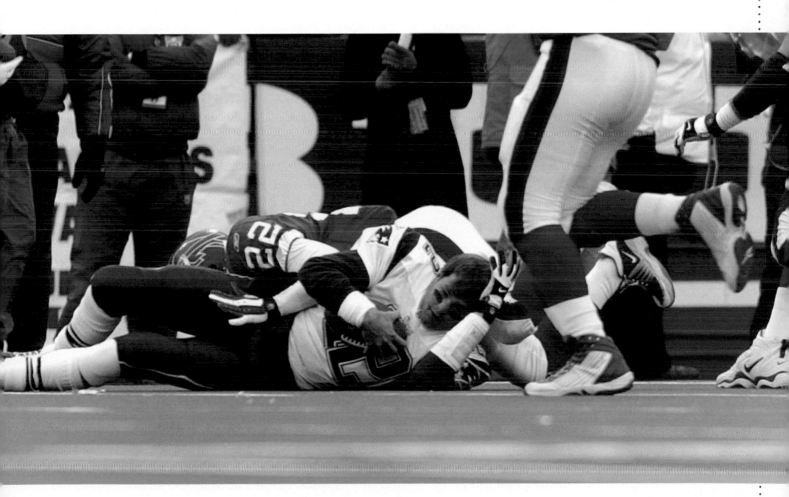

Avoiding Mistakes

By Kevin Mannix

For a quarterback whose game is allegedly limited to dink-and-dunk, nickel-and-dime passes, Tom Brady put up some pretty big numbers yesterday at Foxboro Stadium.

Overall, nothing "unforeseen" occurred to the Patriots' quarterback pro tem during a surprisingly easy 34-17 rout of the Saints. He did what the coaching staff has insisted he would do since he took over the quarterback job nine games ago. Which is why the "foreseeable future" could last a lot longer for Brady than people might expect.

He didn't make any careless or costly mistakes with the ball. He did take sacks and fumbled twice, but the Patriots recovered both of them. He completed 19-of-26 passes for 258 yards, four touchdowns and no interceptions. His quarterback rating for the game was 143.9. Not perfect, but pretty close, and definitely a lot better than even Bill Belichick expected.

The coach, who put his faith—not to mention his future employment—in the hands of a virtual rookie rather than handing it back to Drew Bledsoe, a Pro Bowl player, was typically low-key about Brady's performance.

No gloating.

No predictions of future greatness.

"I thought he played well," the coach said. "He had a good week of practice and a lot of the plays he hit today worked in a similar way to the way they were worked in practice.

"Tom's done a pretty good job every week for nine weeks now. Nothing perfect, but throwing for three or four touchdowns is pretty good."

Obviously, not every game is going to be as good as yesterday's. But from what Brady has shown the coaches through training camp, the preseason and for the last nine games, he's more likely to repeat yesterday's numbers than to put up Trent Green-like stats.

Like his coach, Brady avoided saying anything close to, "I told you so." Instead, he concentrated on the team's success.

"That's what we're capable of doing on offense," Brady said. "There were a lot of big plays using everybody. We ran the ball well, which made the play-action more effective. We got two pass-interference calls. We're starting to really come into our own."

It didn't take long to see that Brady was unfazed by this week's "quarterback controversy" distraction.

Starting at their 15-yard line, the Patriots went 85 yards in six plays to a quick touchdown and a 7-0 lead. There was an 18-yard completion to the always-dependable Troy Brown over the middle. That was followed by a 2-yard dink to Marc Edwards that the fullback turned into a 16-yard gain. After that there was a screen pass to Antowain Smith that became a 41-yard touchdown, thanks to Smith's running after the catch and the blocking of guard Mike Compton and center Damien Woody.

That's the way this offense is designed. Avoid the big mistake. Get rid of the ball quickly.

Keep defenses off-balance with screens and short passes. It was run that way when Bledsoe was playing the first two weeks, and it continues to be in place now.

"There have not been a lot of changes in the offense from the beginning," Belichick said. "Tom started last week. He started this week, and he's probably going to start next week against the Jets. That's the way it was. That's the way it's going to be.

"It's pretty clear-cut."

Absolutely. Against a pretty good, very aggressive Saints defense, the Patriots just went about their rounds, moving the ball, chewing up the clock and lighting up the scoreboard. They controlled the ball for more than 35 minutes, scoring touchdowns on drives of 68, 78, 80, 85 and 93 yards. The key to that kind of production is avoiding turnovers and recognizing your opportunities. Brady did both yesterday.

Legging Out A Win

By Karen Guregian

The "foreseeable" future sure looked like it was upon us yesterday. Tom Brady, much like the Patriots as a whole, was having a miserable afternoon.

He was being harassed and pummeled by oncoming Jets rushers, and when he had time, he couldn't seem to get out of his own way. As first halves go, they don't get much worse than the one our fair Brady produced.

After a three-and-out to open the third quarter, punctuated by defensive tackle Steve Martin tossing Brady to the turf for a third sack, the whispers started. The quarterback controversy that was put to bed weeks before was picking up steam once again.

The "Bring in Bledsoe" sentiments were surely dancing in more than a few heads after seeing the kid look both over-matched and overwhelmed in the first half. Only Brady continued to do what he does best—and that's making Bill Belichick look like a genius.

Yesterday, he accomplished that by staging his best Paul Pierce impression, turning his game around in the second half much like the Celtics forward did Saturday against the Nets. After hitting 5 of 11 passes for 53 yards in the first half, Brady finished with some rather gaudy stats, completing 20 of 28 passes for 213 yards and no interceptions. He essentially nickel-and-dimed the Jets' defense to death, hitting short routes and watching his receivers make the longer gains from there.

But ultimately, Brady wound up burying the Jets with—of all things—his legs. The stat sheet has him gaining no yards on three carries, but his long rush of 2 (1 3/4 to be exact) is the one that officially killed the Jets yesterday, as it allowed the Pats to gain their final first down and kill the clock in the 17-16 win.

To hear Belichick tell it, Brady was near-heroic on third-and-almost-2 from the 41 with 1:46 to play. The Patriots coach called time, brought Brady to the sideline, and asked him to run a quarterback sweep to the right side.

"When I called Tom over, I could see he was in a lot of pain and hurting," Belichick said. "He really wasn't excited when I told him what the play was, but he sucked it up and ran hard and got the first down on what was as good a run as we had all day from probably the last guy you'd expect."

Apparently, Brady had hurt his ribs on an earlier play—and no, Mo Lewis wasn't the culprit, although he did lay into the quarterback pretty good on an incomplete pass.

Brady didn't want to make a big deal of it, saying he fell on top of the ball at some point in the third quarter. Perhaps the best part to this critical sideline pow-wow had Drew Bledsoe essentially telling Brady to, and we're paraphrasing here, just get the damn first down.

"[Belichick] made the call, and I said, 'That's the one you want, huh?'" a smiling Brady recalled. "Then Drew said, 'Just run the ball and get the first down and win the game.' I said, 'all right. Let's do it.' So we called the play and ended up just getting enough for the first down."

Everyone knew that was the ball game right there. As Brady dropped back, looped around and took off to the right, there appeared to be a lot of daylight, only a Jets

defender quickly plugged the gap. Brady even impressed the guys who normally run the ball with his instincts.

"I thought it was going to be a good play for us. Unfortunately, their defensive end got way up field," Patriots fullback Marc Edwards said. "Brady had to cut inside of him, but he's a tough kid. He's shown his toughness game in and game out. He got in there, banged some heads and got that first down. That's what we needed."

He made something out of nothing. That's what Brady did on the play, and what he did in the game.

Somehow, some way, the legend grew.

Still Good Enough

By Ed Gray

Tom Brady yesterday didn't produce the passing efficiency that made him the second-highest-rated quarterback in the NFL by completing more than 70 percent of his passes in the Patriots' previous four games. Though he was intercepted twice and failed to throw a touchdown pass at Foxboro Stadium, the emerging star was pleased with the end result, a 27-16 victory over the Cleveland Browns.

"Now we're 8-5 and just continuing to make progress with this team," said Brady, who completed 19 of 28 passes (67.8 percent) and missed joining Joe Montana as the only quarterbacks with five straight 70 percent games.

"If we continue to do the things we're capable of, to not turn the ball over, to be efficient in the red zone, to be efficient on third down, and the defense continues to play the way they do, we're really going to be something to reckon with," Brady said.

Brady had to reckon with a swarming Browns defense that shut down the Pats' running game until late in the fourth quarter.

"I thought they did a pretty good job of stopping the run. They're pretty stout up front. They had a good D-line, we knew that going in," said the second-year quarterback, who is 8-3 as a starter since replacing an injured Drew Bledsoe. "We were effective at certain points in the passing game and other points not so efficient, not so sharp."

When he had time to throw, Brady was effective, but his efficiency dipped under pressure, particularly in the third quarter when Earl Little intercepted a pass that Brady put up for grabs while being tackled.

"Just a bad play. That's what you say. Sometimes taking a sack isn't all that bad, especially on third and long," said Brady, who was sacked three times and was also intercepted by Corey Fuller in the first quarter. "It was a bad play. You hope those things don't happen again. I think there was another play in the game that something similar happened and I just held the ball."

The Michigan product, who had high praise for wide reciever Troy Brown and the returning Terry Glenn, was happy with the victory, but he strives to become more efficient in the Pats' final three games.

"There were a lot of plays in the second half on offense that we could have taken control of the game and it so happened we left it to the second-to-last drive of the game," Brady said. "As you come down the stretch, you've got to start eliminating mistakes."

QB Controversy Rekindled

By Steve Buckley

Week after week, Tom Brady has been answering the same tired old questions from the same tired old sportswriters.

But late yesterday afternoon, after the Patriots had completed a 12-9, hold-your-breath, overtime victory over the Buffalo Bills, the knights of the keyboard had all kinds of exciting new questions to ask the young quarterback.

Hey, Tom, how many fingers do I have up?

Hey, Tom, do you know who the president of the United States is?

Hey, Tom, do you know what day it is?

To say that Brady got his bell rung yesterday would be the understatement of this over-the-top season. It was a highlight-film hit for the ages, one that the Brady kids, grandkids and great-grandkids will be seeing. And it was delivered by the Bills' 5-foot-9 cornerback, Nate Clements.

Brady landed at the New England 39. His helmet landed in nearby Cheektowaga.

Save for a small mark on his left earlobe—he looked like Manny Ramirez without the Band-Aids—Brady was not injured. But The Kid struggled against the Bills, both before and after Clements measured him for a new scally cap. His performance was reminiscent of Holyfield-Ruiz: He kept failing to connect.

Brady completed 19 of 35 passes for 237 yards, with no touchdowns, and he was constantly overthrowing receivers.

Patriots coach Bill Belichick was given an easy opportunity to dismiss Brady's struggles as nothing more than a young quarterback being thwarted by a dazzling, ingenious defensive scheme. Instead,

Belichick said: "It was him. We weren't efficient throwing the ball. We missed a lot of opportunities."

Sure, Belichick eventually did an end-around and delivered sufficient props to the Buffalo defense.

"They did a good job of taking a lot of things away from us," said Belichick, who also deflected some of the blame from the quarterback by adding, "Their defense did a good job . . . we didn't run the ball particularly well . . . we had trouble on pass protection . . . we didn't convert on third downs."

But it's that first quote—"It was him"—that is guaranteed to have Patriots fans buzzing all week. As the Pats prepare for Saturday's showdown against the Miami Dolphins, fans will be digging into the hope chest and dusting off their old Tom Brady-or-Drew Bledsoe arguments.

You know it and I know it, and, yes, Brady knows it: There will be people calling up the talk shows to fire up the burners to the Quarterback Controversy. Belichick will be asked if maybe, just maybe, Bledsoe will get some extra reps this week at practice. Reporters will stake out Bledsoe's locker, just in case the veteran has something to offer on the subject.

"Well, I know a lot of people are interested in it, but to me it doesn't mean anything," Brady said of the QB controversy. "You just worry about what you can do to get better. I evaluate myself.

"It's what people like to talk about. It's an easy topic and a natural topic. It's part of playing professional football."

Just as Bledsoe has said all the right things, so too has Brady. He continues to supply breezy, upbeat answers to all ques-

tions, and sometimes he's even funny. Yesterday, commenting on the Clements hit, he noted that it didn't hurt much because "[Clements] is just a little guy, not that I'm a big guy or anything."

But he also explained away his high passes by noting that Buffalo's "crown" field—how it's higher in the middle—affected the way he threw. He said he "made some adjustments" for the second half.

Of course, the problem is that he was no more successful in the second half than in the first half.

And admit it: If Bledsoe had played against the Bills yesterday, and struggled, and then offered a rationalization about that dreaded crown field at Ralph Wilson Stadium, he'd be swinging by his ankles from a tree along Route 1.

What happens if Brady struggles against the Dolphins on Saturday?

Until this season is over—be it in two weeks or in the Super Bowl—the Quarterback Controversy lives.

Nice Catch

By Mark Murphy

As he galloped to stay under the first pass of Kevin Faulk's NFL career, Tom Brady finally gained complete respect for his receivers.

The throw—a high, third-and-one lob that Brady would cradle before scooting out of bounds on the Miami 20-yard line—set up Antowain Smith's 2-yard run for the game's first score in a 20-13 victory yesterday over the Miami Dolphins.

It also sparked life not only in the Pats' offense but in what had been a slow start for Brady, who eventually completed 11 of 19 passes for 108 yards and one touchdown.

And, oh yes, one catch for 23 yards. "I don't think I've ever caught a pass," he said. "I told everyone that I turned a touchdown into a 23-yard gain. When I cuss out those receivers now, I'll have a better idea of what they go through."

The pass play was one of those time-sensitive schemes that stayed locked up in offensive coordinator Charlie Weis's playbook for an eternity.

Weis finally saw the opportunity to use it in Miami's man-to-man coverage.

"Charlie made it known as we went out for the game that [the play] would come out pretty quick," said Brady of the play that started with a direct snap to Faulk before the quarterback circled out alone to a completely open left side.

"I just tried not to drop the ball," Brady said.

Indeed, Faulk appeared to be more in his element on the play than Brady. The Patriots' running back actually logged time as a quarterback at Carenoro High in Lafayette, La., and last threw a pass during his junior season in college at LSU.

"I was real excited, but I think Tom was even more excited about the play than me," said Faulk. "Coming out of my hand, it felt like a jump shot. I knew it was there."

Faulk said he saw Miami linebacker Zach Thomas come up. As for the rest of the coverage, "It was wide open. They're a man-to-man team," he said. "I looked up and saw nobody, no one at all."

In other words, the timing couldn't have been better, even if Brady wisely played it safe instead of looking to score.

"It's one of those plays we've had in all year," said Patriots coach Bill Belichick. "Something always seemed to come up, and it wouldn't get called. But [yesterday] was a great situation, and it worked the way we had planned. Charlie made a great call, and Kevin made a great throw.

"It didn't always look that way in practice, I'll say that."

Ready for the Playoffs

By Steve Buckley

The game was a one-sided ho-hummer, played in a near-empty stadium on a cold, misty, dreary North Carolina Sunday.

Final score? Playoff-bound Patriots 38, down-for-the-count Carolina Panthers 6. It was a game that at halftime was closer than it should have been, yet was in the bag by the middle of the third quarter. They could have stopped it there and nobody would have complained—especially the Panthers, who played the game with their cars warming up in the Ericsson Stadium parking lot.

But when Patriots quarterback Tom Brady slid a 5-yard touchdown pass into the waiting mitts of Jermaine Wiggins early in the fourth quarter, you'd have thought it was the play that had propelled New England into the playoffs. Brady threw his arms into the air, and then he ran into the end zone and laid a big ol' bear hug on Wiggins, explaining later: "I'm not even sure what I said to him. Whatever it was, it's probably something you can't print."

Could anybody blame the kid for getting so excited? For most of the day it seemed as though he had been running in place while his teammates were running victory laps around Ericsson Stadium. He was present, but not a presence. So now, finally, he had tossed a touchdown strike, and yeah, you bet, with absolutely no apologies, he danced in the end zone with the Pride of East Boston.

"One of the things I've discovered is that touchdown passes don't come as easy as they did earlier in the year," Brady said." "I'm a pretty emotional guy anyway, so yeah, I wanted to celebrate this one."

It's true that touchdown passes don't come as easy as they did earlier this season. But it's also true that victories continue to flow merrily for the Patriots. With Brady at quarterback, the Pats were 11-3 during the regular season, and they go into the playoffs with six straight wins.

But cynics will argue that while the Patriots are winning WITH Brady, they are not winning BECAUSE of Brady. Now before we go any further, rest assured that you're not going to read an encore of that "Brady vs. Bledsoe" oldie but goodie. As the Patriots prepare for what Bill Parcells dubbed, "The Tournament," be advised that Drew Barrymore has a better chance of seeing game action than Drew Bledsoe.

But these were the keys to victory for the Pats yesterday:

• Defense. The Pats not only kept the Panthers out of the end zone, but they also provided two touchdowns on interception returns by Ty Law (46 yards) and Otis Smith (76 yards).

• Special teams. Troy Brown returned a punt for 68 yards, and Wiggins downed a Ken Walter punt at the Buffalo 1-yard line.

• The running game. Antowain Smith closed out his impressive season with a workmanlike 81 yards on 21 carries, including a 32-yard touchdown.

Brady? The Pro Bowl-bound hotshot . . . the sophomore sensation . . . the Serra slinger . . . was 17 for 29 for 198 yards against a team that closed out the season with an NFL-record 15 consecutive losses. He threw two interceptions.

If you're expecting some kind of hand-wringing or sense of impending doom from Patriots coach Bill Belichick,

forget it. He practically blamed himself for two interceptions by Carolina's Deon Grant, observing that, "We were probably trying to force a few things," and then giving credit to Grant for making great plays.

"And anytime you win a game 38-6, there are enough good things to go around," the coach said. "[Brady] kept us in the game and made improvements."

Translation No. 1: The Patriots won in spite of Brady.

Translation No. 2: He wasn't as bad in the fourth quarter as he was in the first quarter.

And that, Patriots fans, is why Brady was so celebratory after he connected with

Wiggins in the fourth quarter. (By the way, was there anybody in the universe last July who predicted there would be a Tom Brady-to-Jermaine Wiggins touchdown moment during the regular season?) It may not have been the most important touchdown of the season, but it is the touchdown that was no doubt on Brady's mind last night as the playoff-bound Patriots flew back to Boston.

"All you [media] guys have wanted to talk about the playoffs for the last five weeks," Brady said. "Well, now you can talk about it. Bring it on."

A Star is Born— Again

By Karen Guregian

The game was clearly in Tom Brady's hands, which is exactly the way the Oakland Raiders wanted it.

They dared the second-year quarterback, who was making his first appearance in an NFL playoff game, to beat them with his arm. They dared him to pull out a victory in a raging blizzard.

And that's exactly what he did. Brady led the Patriots' magical 16-13 overtime win over the Raiders in the winter wonderland that was Foxboro Stadium last night.

Now read this: There should no longer be even the remotest hint of a quarterback controversy. Tom Brady is The Man. Period.

Brady didn't fold. He didn't play like this was merely the 15th game of his NFL career. He played with the poise of a veteran.

If possible, his legend grew, as he completed 32 of 52 passes for 312 yards in conditions that were more suited to the Iditarod. He didn't throw a touchdown, but he ran for a crucial one—a 6-yard dash—to spark the comeback.

After a mediocre first half (6 for 13, 74 yards and an interception), Brady—largely using the no-huddle offense—picked apart the Raiders, engineering the team's comeback from a 10-point deficit after three quarters. Even with an assist from referee Walt Coleman, who ruled a Brady fumble an incomplete pass after review during the game-tying drive, it was hard to find much fault with the young quarterback's performance.

"That's been his MO the whole year," said offensive lineman Mike Compton. "Everybody's talking about him being a second-year quarterback. Well, he's a student of the game. He's composed. There was never a doubt out there. We never had to go to Tom and say, 'Hey, keep your head up.'

"He's a leader," Compton went on. "He leads with his excitement and also his calmness and poise in the huddle during tight situations."

Brady wasn't just a complementary part of this win. He wasn't there simply to avoid mistakes. He pulled this game out, completing 26 of 39 passes for 238 yards in the second half.

On the controversial fourth-quarter call, Brady dropped back and was hit from the blind side by Charles Woodson. Brady fumbled, and the ball was recovered by Greg Biekert. However, the officials went to the booth for a replay, which showed Brady's arm was back, and appeared to be moving forward at the point he lost the ball.

"Yeah, I was throwing the ball," Brady said with a sheepish grin. "[Woodson] hit me as I was throwing. How do you like that?"

The Raiders didn't like it much, but there was no recourse at that point. The ruling was overturned, giving Brady an incomplete pass instead of a fumble, and the Patriots had new life. Brady then hit David Patten with a 13-yard pass to set up Adam Vinatieri's 45- yarder that tied the game at 13.

After the Pats won the toss in overtime, Brady hit on eight straight passes, using practically every receiver on the field, to set up Vinatieri for the game-winner.

"I think you've got to commend him for the poise he showed under pressure in this situation, handling those tough condi-

tions and just hanging in there because, you know, that's what he does," Pats coach Bill Belichick said of his Pro Bowl quarterback.""He might have a bad play here or there. He certainly had a couple [last night], but he battled right through them and just hung in there and started making some good ones."

Said Vinatieri: "Watching him, you'd think he had 10 years in this league. He just has so much poise. He didn't razzle-dazzle and woo you to death. He just makes plays."

He just wins, as the Raiders found out the hard way.

Still the Man

By Kevin Mannix

Before all the Bledsonians on Planet Patriot get too carried away, remember this: Tom Brady is still the Patriots' quarterback. If, as expected, Brady's twisted ankle recovers sufficiently in the next few days, he will almost certainly be back in the starting lineup when the Patriots take on the Rams in Super Bowl XXXVI next Sunday.

Bledsoe's return to action after nearly four months of inactivity and his role in the Patriots' 24-17 victory over the Steelers in the AFC championship game was another feel-good story. But that's where it's likely to end.

In fact, head coach Bill Belichick admitted that he considered putting Brady back in the lineup in the second half, but he figured a healthy Bledsoe was better than an injured Brady.

Bledsoe did an admirable job given the circumstances. He came off the bench cold and directed the offense to its only touchdown of the game. For somebody who hasn't taken a snap in a game since Sept. 23, he made some very good throws.

But the bottom line is that the Patriots are now Brady's team. The offense that carried the Pats through eight straight wins and into the Super Bowl is dependent on the quarterback making the right decision quickly and then getting rid of the ball even quicker. That's Brady's game, not Bledsoe's.

Coming into the game in relief of Brady in the second quarter, Bledsoe did complete 10 of 21 passes, including three gems—an 11-yard touchdown pass to David Patten, a 15-yard dart to Charles Johnson over the middle and a clutch 18-yard floater to Troy Brown on third and 12 in the fourth quarter.

But he also made a couple of horrendous mistakes at critical junctures of the game.

Early in the third quarter, the Pats had a chance to pad their lead beyond 14-3 when Tedy Bruschi recovered a Kordell Stewart fumble at the Steelers' 35. On third and 7 from the 32, Deshea Townsend was caught holding Troy Brown, an infraction that should have given the Pats a first down at the Pitt 27. Unfortunately, on the same play, Bledsoe was flagged for an intentional grounding penalty when he flipped a blind pass over the middle of the field to avoid a sack.

In the fourth quarter, with the Pats holding a 24-17 lead, Bledsoe either misread the Steeler coverage or made a terrible throw. Regardless, he hit Pittsburgh linebacker Joey Porter in the hands at the Pats' 21.

Those are the kind of mistakes the Patriots have been avoiding through their run to the Super Bowl. They're also the kinds that Bledsoe should never make, even with all his recent inactivity.

Brady's numbers weren't spectacular, and he did miss Patten on a long pass early in the game, but he avoided bad decisions that could have changed momentum.

Bledsoe obviously understands his place in the pecking order, but he's also holding out hope that he'll get another chance at quarterbacking a Super Bowl champion.

"This is the biggest game there is," he said.

"Everybody wants to play in this game. [Not playing] would be a hard situation.

"When the team is winning and you're watching, you feel satisfaction because you're helping and you're throwing scout-team balls and helping with game plans and all that kind of stuff. But you play this game to play. It feels that much sweeter when you're on the field."

But the bottom line is that while Belichick may have accidentally discovered Brady, he knows the kind of quarterback he wants to run his offense.

That's Brady.

Primetime Drivetime

By Rich Thompson

The Patriots' game-winning drive went 53 yards on nine plays and can be summed up in three letters.

M-V-P.

Patriots quarterback Tom Brady, at age 24 and in his first season as a starter, secured his place in Super Bowl folklore by mounting the game-winning drive that beat the St. Louis Rams, 20-17, in Super Bowl XXXVI Sunday night in New Orleans.

Kurt Warner tied the game at 17 on a 26-yard scoring pass to Ricky Proehl with 1:37 to play. The Patriots got the ball on their own 17 with 1:21 to play and no timeouts in the bank. Even to the likes of John Elway and Joe Montana, the prospects of success would have seemed bleak against a Rams defense that had held the Pats scoreless in the second half.

But playing it safe was not an option the Patriots could explore.

"The thought never crossed my mind," said Brady. "Coach came over and said, 'We are going to go for the win here.'"

Though Brady's numbers (16 for 27, 145 yards) did not apporach Kurt Warner's (28-44, 365 yards), Brady's self-assurance resonated through the huddle on the drive. He then set in motion the sequence of events that would result in the first Super Bowl title in Patriots history.

"Tom was just like normal," said guard Joe Andruzzi. "He has a lot of confidence in himself and he brought that confidence into the huddle. We just knew deep down the offense was going to go out and get the job done."

Operating out of the shotgun, Brady opened the drive with a 5-yard flare pass to J. R. Redmond, and that set the stage for the drama to unfold. Redmond would record the drive's first three receptions for 24 yards and two first downs.

Brady completed 5 of 8 for 53 yards. The biggest play was a 23-yarder to Troy Brown to the Rams' 36. A quick 6-yard hit to tight end Jermaine Wiggins moved

the ball to the Rams' 30. Brady spiked the ball to stop the clock with seven seconds remaining.

"We gained some yards on the first play and it kept going," said Brady. "I hit Troy, I mean, the best receiver in the league as far as I'm concerned."

Adam Vinatieri then stepped onto the world stage and delivered a 48-yard field goal as time expired to cap the drive and make Super Bowl history.

Rewards Come By Truckload for MVP

By George Kimball

The sleek black Escalade EXT with which Tom Brady was presented yesterday carries a sticker price of almost $50,000, not including delivery charge. But if Super Bowl XXXVI's Most Valuable Player walked up to the Hertz counter and asked for the same vehicle this morning, they'd take one look at his driver's license and tell him to come back in August when he was old enough to rent one.

All in all, the Cadillac won't make a bad ride for a kid who's been tooling around Foxboro in a pickup truck for the past year.

"It's actually a Cadillac truck," Brady pointed out. "I got the best of both in that. I'm not sure where that car is going. I need something to drive back home in California. I'm not on my dad's meal ticket anymore."

Not much chance of that happening. The young Pats quarterback might have spent the past six months living out a fairy tale, but he's about to be rewarded for it.

Salaries of today's NFL stars being what they are, the tangible rewards of winning a championship are usually like so many Mardi Gras beads to your average Super Bowl MVP. A winning player's share might be impressive to you and me, but it's what some of these guys hand out in tips over the course of a year. And as for the obligatory Disney World trip, well, it might be nice to take the kids down for a few days.

For Tom Brady, on the other hand, the $100,000-plus in postseason loot he picked up between the playoffs and Sunday night's win at the Superdome represented more than a third of what he earned in salary this season. The SUV he picked up yesterday is worth $12,000 more than the signing bonus he got from the Patriots when he was drafted two years ago.

And Disney World? I mean, can't you just picture Tom Brady, a baseball cap jauntily turned backward atop his head, grinning from ear to ear as he personally samples Mr. Toad's Wild Ride?

Well, perhaps not yesterday.

"I don't know if I have the stomach I used to have when I was a kid," Brady confessed. "So nothing that goes around and around. . . . Hey, is there a Ferris wheel at Disney World?"

In truth, Brady feels as if he's been whirling through Space Mountain this season.

"As far as I'm concerned, the emotional ride has been straight up," he said. "There hasn't been a downer yet, except this morning at about 6 a.m. when the alarm went off. Other than that, it's been pretty awesome."

There hadn't been much time for sleep. From the moment Adam Vinatieri's 48-yard field goal split the uprights in the most thrilling Super Bowl in football annals, there had been a seemingly endless round of interviews. It was nearly midnight by the time Brady returned to the Fairmont Hotel, where he partied into the wee hours of the morning with his family and friends before being dragged off to yesterday's MVP presentation.

NFL commissioner Paul Tagliabue, who presented Brady with his hardware, recalled that on their way to the Superdome on Sunday, Hall of Fame quarterback Roger Staubach had presciently noted, "You can't go into the Super Bowl

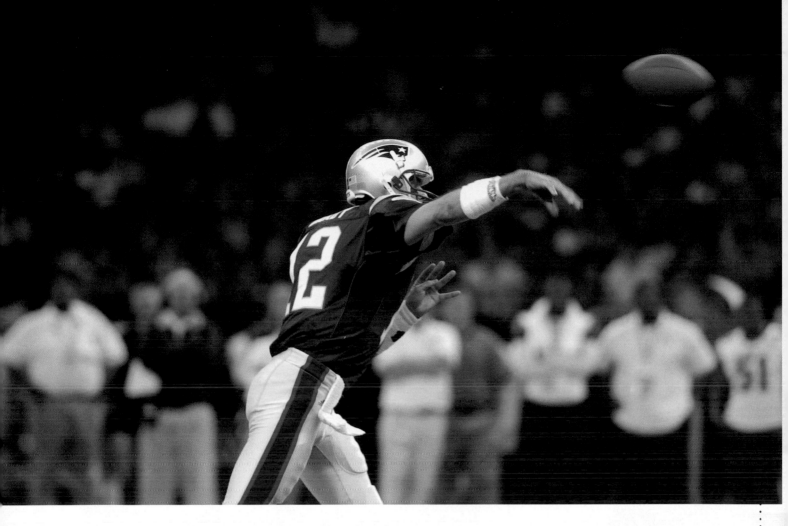

with the slightest doubt, and the thing I love about this young quarterback is he's so mentally tough, so confident and such a leader."

Brady is all of those things, of course, at least in part because he doesn't know any better.

One football type presented Brady with a riddle yesterday: When the Super Bowl has been played one week after the conference championships, the underdog team has won 4 of 6 times. When the game has been played two weeks later, the favored team almost always wins, usually in a blowout.

"Why do you think that is?" Brady was asked.

"Beats the hell out of me," he replied with disarming candor, and the room erupted with laughter.

In the meantime, he is going to find himself fielding so many endorsement offers he'll have to hire somebody just to sift through them all. Reminded yesterday

that he's going to be asked to pose for covers and endorse products he's never heard of, Brady broke into another grin.

"I'm working on it," he said. "This is all new to me, and I'm like a kite in the wind. Right now I'm just going with the flow. But I'm working on it."

The comparisons between Brady's 2001 season and Kurt Warner's Cinderella ride in 1999 have been well chronicled. Like Warner then, Brady played for the NFL minimum for a second-year player this season and earned less than $300,000. He is on the books next year to earn $377,833, but he's going to make a lot more than that. Sometime between now and April, or whenever the team trades away Drew Bledsoe, the Patriots will ensure the security of their investment by signing Brady to a long-term extension, and the $5 million signing bonus Warner got after his Super Bowl win two years ago ought to be a good place to start.

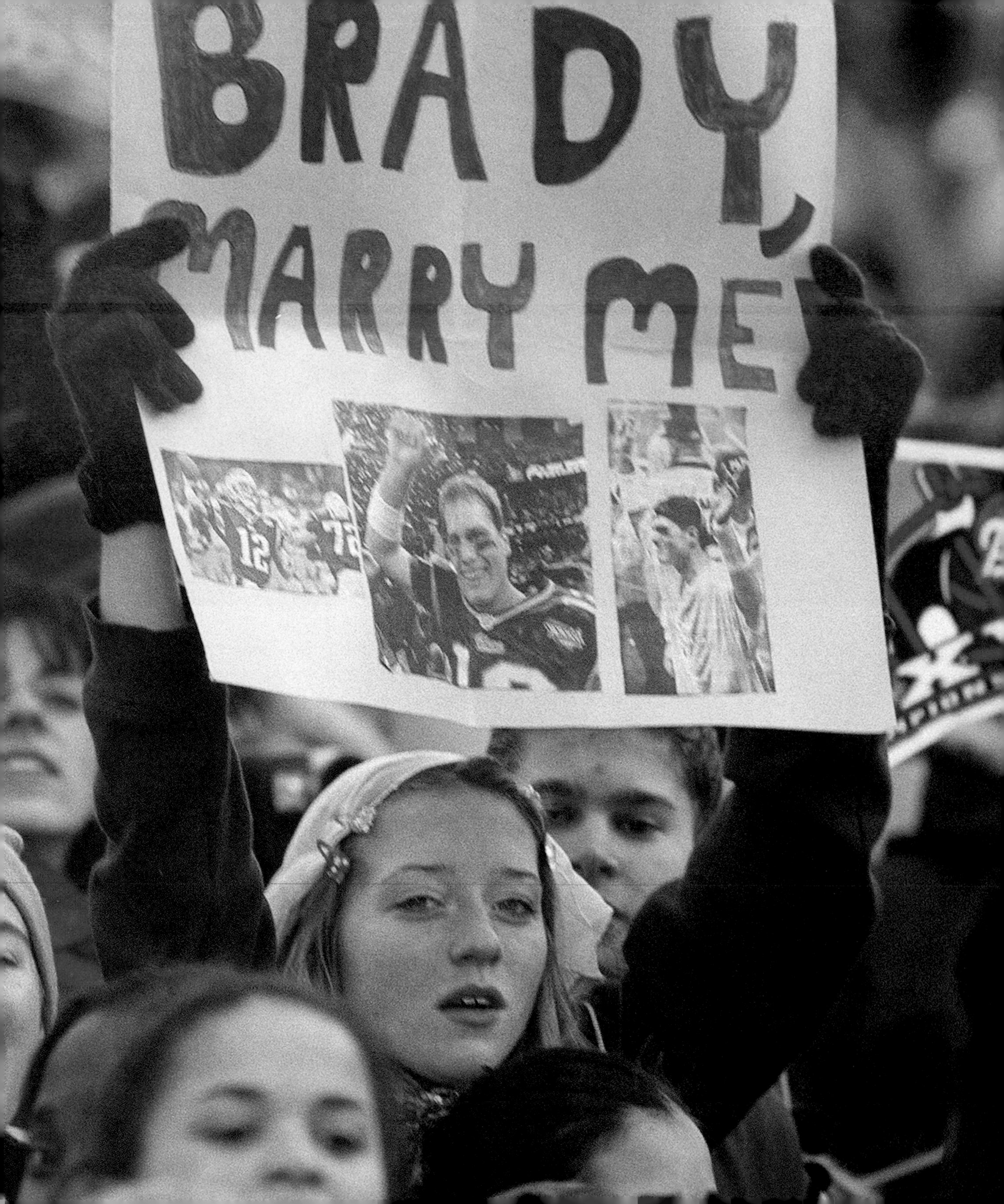
BRADY,
MARRY ME

Kid Stuff Not a Passing Concern

By Dave Reardon

Some went straight for the cell phone. Others tried to run to the locker room.

But Tom Brady headed directly to the wheelchairs.

"Hey, my man's got my jersey on," Brady said by way of introduction. "How you doing?"

The real answer is not very good. But today, the kid with terminal leukemia is as happy as Brady, the Super Bowl hero who is sharing his joy with those all around him.

For many of the players after AFC Pro Bowl practice yesterday at Aloha Stadium, it was time to make plans for the evening or negotiate the obstacle course of fans and media as quickly as possible.

But Brady, Mr. Efficiency on the field, chose to take his time, spending time—real time—with the Make-A-Wish kids. After all, there were minds to change.

"You guys are all Badger fans? We might have to convert you to Wolverines fans," Brady, the former Michigan quarterback, said to several seriously ill but beaming children from Wisconsin.

Brady didn't just scribble his name and run away. He chatted with them for a good 10 minutes. He learned their names, their favorite foods, whom else they had met on this sunny day in their gray lives.

It was real and unforced. Like Brady on the field.

Like Kurt Warner, Brady is the star who seemingly came out of nowhere. Actually, Warner's story of previous employment at an Iowa supermarket is more melodramatic, especially compared to Brady's background of coming from one of the nation's most prominent college football programs.

But Brady, so far, is every bit the aw-shucks All-American good guy, in word and action.

His emergence on the field, after Drew Bledsoe's injury in the second game of the season, may not have been riveting, but it was steady. Around him each game, Pats stars seemed to materialize—kicker Adam Vinatieri, bruising rusher Antowain Smith, defensive cogs Ty Law, Lawyer Milloy & Co.—while Brady quietly but effectively did his job. And always, he was quick to heap credit on his teammates.

On the field, Warner is generally more spectacular, while Brady thrives on letting the game come to him one little play at a time.

"He's a very confident guy and he doesn't make mistakes," Patriots receiver Troy Brown said. "He studies hard, works hard, does all the right things."

Everything Brady does on the field is with a purpose.

"He appears to make quick reads," said Rams defensive back Aeneas Williams. "He's decisive. He knows what he wants to do. You could see his confidence progress as the season went along. He's able to deliver the ball accurately. That's the No. 1 thing."

Colts receiver Marvin Harrison said Brady is refreshing.

"Being as young as he is, he still realizes it's a game," Harrison said. "You can see it in his face that he knows it's about having fun more than putting undue pressure on yourself."

On this sunny day in Hawaii, Brady seemed to understand real pressure is living in a wheelchair and wondering how many months, weeks or days you have left. With the demands all around him, the Make-A-Wish kids had his full attention.

"They deserve it like anyone else, more so," he said.

"I'll do anything for those kids."

Super Journey

By Kevin Mannix

Two months after the title was earned, the fact that he and his teammates are Super Bowl champions still hasn't hit Patriots quarterback Tom Brady. Not totally, anyway.

"It's been tough to sit down and think about things so far," Brady said yesterday at CMGI Field. "There has been one continuous string of things. Even going to the White House (Tuesday), it didn't hit me that we're champions. Maybe because I'm young and naive. Being there was great, but you feel like a tourist. Maybe once we get the Super Bowl ring. That's when I might get the feeling. So far, though, I don't really have it."

Brady's "continuous string" has been pretty impressive. A Super Bowl championship. An MVP award and the accompanying visit to Disney World. A victory parade in Boston. A trip to the Pro Bowl in Hawaii. Judging beauty contests. Golf at Pebble Beach.

And he was one of many Patriots to throw out the ceremonial first pitch during the Opening Day festivities for the Red Sox at Fenway Park.

"I was like a kid throwing out the first ball with the other guys," Brady said. "Coming out from under the flag and walking in from left field was like going through the tunnel onto the field at the Super Bowl."

The team also visited the White House, where the players shook hands and took pictures with President George W. Bush.

"I was just a little awestruck standing beside the most powerful man in the world," Brady said. "It's been great. All of it. But you know, the best thing I've done in the last two months was that Super Bowl. Everything else has been fun but nothing like winning the Super Bowl."

His reaction to the win showed that. Just after Adam Vinatieri's 48-yard field goal split the uprights to give the Pats a 20-17 victory and the first championship in franchise history, the camera caught a wide-eyed Brady pounding Drew Bledsoe on the chest in celebration. Reading his lips was no problem. "We won!" he said.

Brady was Joe Montana cool during the final drive that led up to Vinatieri's kick. Once the kick was good, he became a raving celebrant.

Everybody saw it. Everybody appreciated the legitimate unbridled euphoria. Everybody except Brady. He needed to see a tape of the game to realize what he had done.

"I don't remember doing that," said Brady, who admitted to other gaps in his immediate postgame memory. "You do lose it at some point. The ball went through and the next thing I remember was being in the locker room. I think back to the game and wonder what I did on the field afterward. I don't remember who I was hugging. I'm still trying to get back that hour. People had to tell me who was hugging who and who was doing what.

"Watching the celebration on tape was great. I love watching the guys celebrate. Ty [Law] jumping on Otis [Smith's] back. Stuff like that. It was great."

Now it's back to work. Brady and the rest of the players have begun their off-season workouts. Four days a week of running and lifting weights and attending meetings. The season may be five months away, but . . .

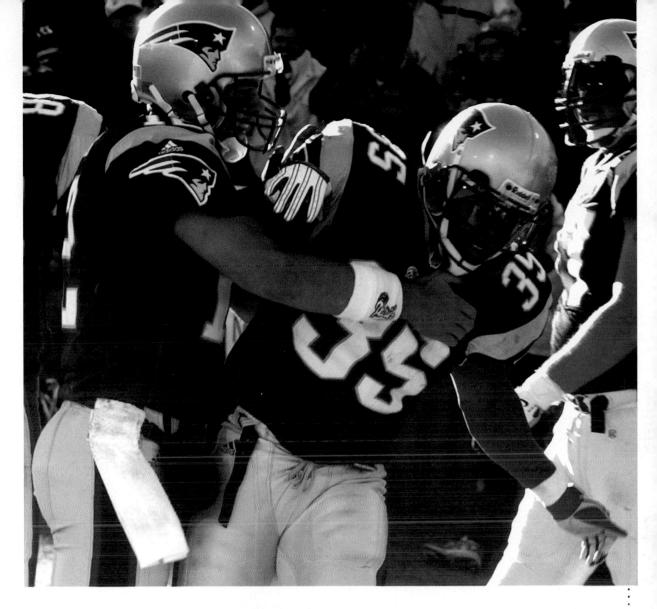

"This is where it starts for us," Brady said. "It's a new season and a fresh start. A lot of other teams have already put their [2001] seasons behind them. We have to do the same. We know what made us successful. Now how can we build on that? We understand that we're the hunted now. We have to step it up because we're going to get everybody's best shot when we play.

"Personally, there's a ton of work to do. I know there will be a lot of distractions, things that could take away from what I'm trying to be as a player. What's really important to me is being a great quarterback. I'm not going to let anything get in the way of that."

The Patriots continue to add veteran free agents to their 2002 roster, agreeing to terms with three more yesterday.

Cornerback Tom Knight will receive a two-year contract worth $1.65 million. The 6-foot, 195-pound former first-round pick out of Iowa spent his first five seasons with the Arizona Cardinals, who didn't attempt to re-sign him because of his injury problems.

The Pats also reached agreement with unrestricted free agents Steve Martin and Ryan Phillips. Martin, a defensive tackle, recorded a career-high 40 tackles for the Jets last season. Phillips, a linebacker, played in 13 games for the Colts in 2001 and was a member of the Giants' Super Bowl XXXV team.

The Pats released safety Mark Washington and defensive end Cecil Deckard.

Brady Takes Keys

By Michael Felger

Tom Brady showed up in Foxboro yesterday morning just as he has every day since the beginning of the off-season conditioning program three weeks ago, only this time it had to feel a little different. With Drew Bledsoe traded to Buffalo, Brady is on his own.

Brady was immediately presented with an interview request to discuss his new status. He declined, which is just the same. The Patriots and their fans know the score.

This is now—formally, officially and unequivocally—Brady's team.

How will he react?

"I don't think he's really worried about it. He never has been," said veteran teammate Willie McGinest. "He just goes out and plays. He's already done what nobody else has done. So that pressure is over. He won a Super Bowl in his second year. The only question is whether he can do it again."

Early indications are that little has changed for Brady. He's still putting in his off-season work and is a fixture in the weight room. He's working his way down a list of items he needs to improve on, presented by his coaches earlier in the offseason. Despite a bevy of high-profile engagements following the Super Bowl—Disney World, the Miss America Pageant, the Oscars, a *Sports Illustrated* photo shoot—Brady has kept a low profile since returning to New England.

And yet the pressure remains. He no longer has a three-time Pro Bowl quarterback pushing him for the job on the field or counseling him off it. He no longer has the benefit of anonymity. He'll soon be presented with a multi-year, multi-million-dollar contract. The Patriots will be in prime time all autumn and the expectations will be out of this world.

Of course, Brady faced similar pressures last year, and everyone knows how that turned out. It's why his teammates aren't exactly fretting over how the 24-year-old reigning Super Bowl MVP will respond.

"He's handled the pressure well," McGinest said. "He's relaxed. He's a fighter. He has a lot of heart and he doesn't back down. ... I think he's going to be up to the challenge. I think he's going to play great. We all have confidence in him. He's only going to get better."

The competition with Bledsoe surely made Brady a better player last year. It's impossible to know how Brady will react to not having that competition this year, but he at least has to realize the following: No job is safe on Belichick's Patriots.

Bledsoe, arguably the most important player in the history of the organization, lost his job last year. So did Bryan Cox. So did Ted Johnson. So did everyone else who got hurt, failed to hold up their end of the bargain or help the team win football games.

Translation: If Brady struggles for an extended period of time next year and the Pats start losing, no one should be shocked to see Damon Huard under center.

"I'm not sure we've eliminated his competition," said director of player personnel Scott Pioli, who expects to add a fourth quarterback to the roster, former Texas star Major Applewhite. "I wouldn't agree with that at all. I think Tom is a self-

motivated guy. But only time will tell how that impacts him."

Of course, if the Pats had brought Bledsoe back for competition, it would have been accompanied by a media circus and daily distractions in the locker room. Both Belichick and Pioli have refused to publicly admit it, but it's hard to imagine that that prospect wasn't a factor.

One clear indication is the timing of the deal. The Bills were offering considerations for the 2003 draft, creating no urgency to get the trade done during the 2002 draft weekend. In theory, the Pats could have waited until the trading deadline in October, working the market for a better deal.

Instead, the Pats jumped when Buffalo—a bitter divisional rival who appears on the schedule twice a year—finally met their price. There was no hesitation. The Pats got their unconditional first-round pick and now the slate is clean. The distraction is gone.

When asked, Pioli would only say, "We felt it was a fair deal for everyone involved. It was the time to do the deal."

Were the Pats worried about Bledsoe making life difficult if he were still on the team? Pioli said no way.

"I don't think that Drew Bledsoe is ever a guy you have to worry about," Pioli said. "He'd never do anything to be disruptive. But anything like that is speculation. None of us know what would have happened."

Whether the Pats are better or worse for Bledsoe's departure is one of the many questions fans will be asking themselves as the Pats attempt to defend their Super Bowl title next season. Only Brady can answer it.

Tom Brady: MVP
Most Valuable Patriot

The following photographers from the staff of the
Boston Herald Photography Department contributed to this book.
We gratefully acknowledge the efforts of:

Mike Adaskaveg
Tara Bricking
John Cummings
Renee Dekona
Robert Eng
Michael Fein
Ted Fitzgerald
Mark Garfinkel
David Goldman
Jon Hill
Nancy Lane
Jim Mahoney
George Martell
Ren Norton
Michael Seamans
Matt Stone
Kuni Takahashi
Matthew West
Patrick Whittemore
John Wilcox
Kevin Wisniewski
Darlene Sarno, *Technical support*

Jon Landers, *Chief Photographer*
Ted Anchor, *Assistant Director of Photography*
Arthur Pollack, *Assistant Director of Photography*
Garo Lachinian, *Director of Photography*